Painting Life with Words of Encouragement

Tony Amico

Acknowledgements

First and foremost, to my wife, Valerie, I love her dearly. She saved all I've written over 18+ years. She is my greatest fan. Her love for me and belief in my ability is my greatest inspiration. I thank you for your incredible dedication to editing, conference calls, follow-ups, and countless hours devoted to this project.

To Laura and Al Summa for recognizing and encouraging my ability to bring it to the attention of Laura Ranger, my publisher. To the entire staff of *Foundations* for believing in me as a writer. All contributed in a patient and professional manner without whose input, this book would never materialize in this form. be, Laura Ranger, Steve Soderquist, Toni Michelle, Susan James Pierce, and Dawne Dominique.

I'm compelled to acknowledge my first wife, Nancy, my son Michel's mom. We shared in the joy of having Michel. Regardless of the circumstances, I'll always honor and respect her for giving us the blessing that was Michelangelo. Thank you and God bless you, Nancy.

Mayra, for her loyalty, love and commitment. She is without question, as close to a daughter as I'll ever have.

My cousin, Michele for her 'sister-like' love, her compassionate approach to my endeavors, and her intuitive instinct with regard to my emotions.

I thank those in support of me, as well as those who didn't. I've used all of you and your experiences as fuel for my creative engine. Also, I wanted to add that music has been a great love in my life and a great contributor of ideas to inspire me.

To my art teachers, Jane Brier and Elaine Neuriter. Jane was the first to label me 'an artist' and taught me to strive in everything I do. Writing wasn't even on my radar as a youth.

To Sam D'Andrea, my greatest mentor. He taught me more than Masonry (my trade). He showed me how to recognize my flaws and always improve myself and in Sam's words "strive to create the illusion of perfection," knowing full well all man creates is flawed to some extent.

Foundations Books Publishing
Brandon, MS 39047
www.FoundationsBooks.net

Painting Life with Words of Encouragement
By Tony Amico
ISBN: 978-1726289344

Copyright © 2018 Tony Amico

Cover by Dawné Dominique Copyright © 2018

Edited and Formatted by: Laura Ranger

Published in the United States of America

Worldwide Electronic & Digital Rights

Worldwide English Language Print Rights

All rights reserved. No part of this book may be reproduced, scanned or distributed in any form, including digital and electronic or mechanical, including photocopying, recording, or by any information storage and retrieval system, without the prior written consent of the Publisher, except for brief quotes for use in reviews.

This is primarily a work of non-fiction. Most names characters, businesses, places, events, and incidents are in no way intended to harm nor hurt. All are from significant events and memories of the author at various times throughout his life. The two short stories are purely fictional. Any resemblance to places, names or events to those living or dead are simply coincidental.

Dedication

To my son, Michelangelo Amico who possesses the greatest love in my heart. There is no equal besides my God. Although I've lived the longest portion of my life without Michel being physically present, he may have passed at such a tender age, but he remains within me. In my heart. In my mind. In every fiber of my being.

There is no question his death brought forth the life of my writing. What was once a form of self-therapy and often still is, now has allowed me to share with others on his behalf as well as my own. We remain a part of one another. He is never absent.

To my mom, Angela, my sister, Joann, and brother, Sam for their loving support. Especially to my mom for her influence on me with regard to a positive approach to all circumstances.

To my grandparents, Salvatore and Josephine Amico, Michael and Ida Delfino, and my dad, Anthony Amico (now also deceased). I hope I've made them as proud of me as I am to be a part of them.

To my absolutely incredible army of friends, **all** know full well whom I'm referring to, but should I err and leave one out in my listing of those closest to me I could never forgive myself.

And to all my family members, be it married into or through blood, I love you all and consider myself greatly blessed to be so richly related.

Table of Contents

Lines of Wisdom 1
Time 7
Sunrise 8
Essentials 9
Passing Time 10
Summer 11
End of Summer 12
Winds of Time 13
Tomorrow 14
The Visit 15
Life 17
Peace in the Garden 18
Share 19
High School 20
Step Forward 21
Backup 22
Life's Concert 23
Dark and Lonely Path 24
Given 25
Service 26
Why 27
Five-Year Plan 28
Wooden Box 29
Lesson 30
Our Thinking 31
Puzzles 32

Open Door	34
Empty or Full	35
Life's Meaning	36
Thread of Life	37
Encouragement	38
Priceless	39
Faith Full	40
For the Young and Hungry	41
Be Yourself	42
Naivety	43
Blessed	44
Storm Clouds	46
Victor	47
Therapy in Iron	48
Tragic	49
Losses and Gains	50
A Horse Called Life	51
Family	53
Marbles	55
The Footprints	56
Once a Dad	57
Book of Faces	58
Pets	59
Great Danes	60
Coal	61
Grandpa	62
Grandmother	63
Grandma Amico	64

Grandma's Hugs 66
Cousin 67
Personal 69
Once Again 70
These Hands 71
Anapra 72
The Baby 73
Speeding 74
Sewers 75
The Funeral 76
Masonry by the Book 77
Awards Night Speech 78
Kindergarten 80
Letters 83
A Birthday Note to My Wife 84
Tim 85
Ida and Mike 86
Short Stories 89
Joe, from Forty Fort 91
Alone 99
About the Author 111
More from Foundations 116

Wisdom
A capacity of the mind that allows us to understand life from God's perspective. From Proverbs, Solomon says those who get wisdom love life (Prv 19:8); that it's better to get wisdom than gold (Prv 16:16); and that those who get wisdom find life and receive favor from the Lord (Prv 8:32-35).

Desire wisdom
The second step to getting wisdom is to desire it with all our heart. As Solomon says, we must "look for it as for silver and search for it as for hidden treasure" (Prv 2:4).

Painting Life with Words of Encouragement

Lines of Wisdom

"Relentless," isn't a bad thing. Just be sure you are consistent. People respect that. I tend to look at it as, "Ambition with an attitude."

Ambition can't be taught.

You can take all the negative influences in your life and learn how to turn them into a positive. Or you can become part of the negativity yourself. It's called, *free will*.

Success defined, is peace of mind. It cannot be bought or earned. But *acceptance* is certainly in the equation.

Sometimes it's best to watch things play out. And say nothing.

I've seen the day when "The Magic is Gone," in one's life. Don't resist it, when it beckons to return.

The greatest gift of all is *faith*. For this, I am eternally grateful!

If all you look for is the bad, it's all you'll see.

We mustn't waste time on those who couldn't care less about us. There are so many individuals worthy of our time.

Summer has slipped away, Fall ain't gonna stay. Short, cold days are moving in fast. Hope for a mild winter that won't last.

Don't let the veil of today's problems prevent you from grasping the fabric that is your life. There's so much precious material to wrap yourself up with.

When it all comes down to honesty. It's really all that matters. Isn't it?

You may not be what others expected. But you can do the unexpected for others.

You can backslide or stand tall. The decision is yours to make.

Better to have a little of everything, then a lot of anything.

Everything starts with a *dream*.

We may never agree. And that's okay. My opinion doesn't need justification.

Sometimes we make the right decisions in what others may view as, for the wrong reasons. If it's the right reason in your heart, *it's right*.

Dawn just minutes away. A new day about to play. Planned or spontaneous. What will it be? Come what may for you and me. Looking forward to the first face that I see.

God doesn't test you. He knows what you're capable of withstanding. Best part is, He's taught me about myself.

There is something *good* in every *bad* thing. It may take a while to notice or understand it. But it's there, always.

Your faith will be tested now and then. Will you pass or fail?

If you notice all you've lost more than what you've gained in life. You're likely to lose more. Snap out of it and smile.

We "want," as children. We "desire," as adults. We "need," as we mature. We are "grateful," as we age. If we've "*learned*," along the way.

If I believe it in my heart, there's no changing my mind.

Sometimes you have to catch a curve ball. Be ready.

Business was so much easier when I had a Kool-Aid stand and a cigar box.

Painting Life with Words of Encouragement

Turning in for the night. Was thinking about my life. What would I do differently? I'd live it slower.

Wishing you were something you're not is time *wasted*. Improving what you are is, time *invested*.

My grandparent's blood is on the surface of my existence.

Optimism is a great word. *Determination* is just as good. But *ambition* is a blessing. Have a bright tomorrow.

I listened for the sound of your voice laughing, but I could only hear my own voice crying.

Tony Amico

Painting Life with Words of Encouragement

Time

Sunrise

$\mathcal{A}$s I view this glorious sunrise today, I'm reminded of all the ones I missed when I was blinded and consumed by the veil of anger or despair. Those times are too easy to recall, unfortunately. But then again, if I had not ever experienced darkness. How would I appreciate light? May we enjoy the brightness of every moment today. Even in struggles we are moving forward.

Essentials

Stop before you start your day. *Think* of someone you love. *Pray* for someone else's need. *Give thanks* for those who've done this for you. Step outside and cast your first gaze upward, because all that is bestowed upon you is coming from that direction, whether you believe it or not. I am *grateful* to be one who *believes.*

Passing Time

*P*assing time is difficult for us to deal with often. A year goes by in a flash. An era we wish to relive. And certainly, the loved ones we wish were traveling through this journey with us who are no longer here. During the difficult days, we reach out to those who are still available. Those we can count on. Those who understand. Feel. Hurt. Care. And identify. A piece of music brings unexpected tears. A memory of something said, brings a smile or laughter. Let's not forget, "This is our time." Something we say or do will have an impact on someone after we've passed on. What memory would you like to be part of? Whose life will you influence in such a way that they would wish for one more moment with you? Holiday seasons will come and go... It may be the last for any one of us. Perhaps me. Or you. Be sure that wherever you are standing on the "street corner of life," you won't go unnoticed, forgotten, dismissed, or unappreciated. Just as the one around the next turn or bend in this "glorious road" we are traveling. Savor the moment in time that is *yours* and *theirs*. We are part of both.

Summer

So, the lilac scent of spring has passed. Along with the early sprouts of those colorful tulips. As a matter of fact, all the family of spring flowers have left for another year. The summer has arrived in the form of a long day. Storms releasing the day's heat. The fresh smell of a rain-soaked walkway leading to a lawn, which seems to grow by the minute. We're in the seventh month. Just a dozen or so weeks till fall. If only I could freeze one day and enjoy it for all it's worth. Use every precious moment until I've drained and absorbed all the best parts without missing a bit of a glorious summer day. Oh, wait a minute...I can.

Tony Amico

End of Summer

We're probably seeing the last of Summer days, this week. Take time to breathe it all in. I'm not a winter guy. Not at all. But I suppose Winter is why I appreciate Summer so much. The shortened days are upon us. And soon, the holiday season. Hopefully, the closeness of family and friends will make the long nights seem shorter. This is a time when I look farther ahead, already. Before the first snowflake falls, my eyes are searching for Spring. Too bad I can't hibernate.

Winds of Time

They are like voices caught in the winds of time. Sometimes, like the breeze in the summer, they touch the face of our hearts. They aren't as they were. They are so much more now. And we are so much less without them. That same wind will whisk us away too, someday. And those we leave behind will hear our voices too. Sometimes brisk. Sometimes soft. Always moving us to tears. Soon to be dried by the breeze of life.

Tomorrow

Do you know someone named tomorrow? He seems to always come around midnight. Sometimes to finish what he started yesterday. Sometimes to put off to another day. There are those who may not see tomorrow ever again. That's sad, because he was hanging out with a fella named yesterday just a short time ago. Well it's been nice talking to you. But I have a lot to do. By the way, my name is today. I haven't time to waste.

The Visit

The summer's grass was bathed in the wash of a morning sunrise.

A tree served my back, as I took a seat and closed my eyes.

It was then when I noticed your presence about me leaning in so near.

The sound of your movement such as a breeze wafting past my ear.

I reached out and felt your face in my hands,

your cheeks in my palms, my thumb tracing your brow.

It was as if long ago were alive and present now.

You're here! It's you! Dare I open my eyes?

I try to speak your name but cry out bleating sighs.

Pulling you to my chest, my fingers through your hair.

Your scent within my being since last I held you there.

The breeze turns to a gust, the clouds now hiding the sun.

I grasp at more time to be with you, there is none.

My eyes are open and searching in vain.

My voice cracked and broken as my heart as I call out your name.

Arms now empty at my side.

The sun no longer behind the clouds to hide.

The warming rays on my face.

I continue aimlessly looking for a trace.

And there before me in the soft dirt at my feet,

Are your footprints right where I had taken my seat?

I press my hands to the imprint as if you still were here.

Although I cannot see you, I know that you are near.

The days of sun well come and go. As do our lives they too shall pass,

But till that time when I too am a memory, yours will ever last.

Tony Amico

Painting Life with Words of Encouragement

Life

Tony Amico

Peace in the Garden

There truly is *peace in the garden*.
You work the soil.
No one interferes.
They see you sweat, no need to join in.
You plant the seed, tend it every day, wait for the little sprout.
Then a flower, eventually a yield of something to delight your senses.
To reward your efforts.
And give increasing reason to rest in the garden every day.
Shouldn't our whole life be viewed as, *the garden*?
Every aspect needs tending.
All efforts bring more than it takes.
Patience is a wonderful seed to plant.

My Garden 2018

Share

Within the fullness of life, you will "Sustain and wallow",

"Indulge and endure", "Embrace and reject", "Rejoice and despair. But most of all, you will have *lived* and you hopefully, would have learned it is a blessing to have experienced a life full of all that's offered, bestowed, brought upon you, left at your feet, set on your shoulders, entered in your heart, and enriched you to the point where it is your obligation to share your *spirit* of life with others.

High School

For the High schoolers, please give your best efforts in all you do, for yourself. Knuckle down, suck it up, listen, be kind, help others, and ask for help when you need it. Show respect. Earn respect. Make your mark. Stand out. Stand tall. Be confident, become the dream you have of yourself. Get noticed for the right reasons. You are indeed worthy of your effort. You are loved and admired by your greatest fans, your family. And some of your closest family may not even be related. Bond with friendship. Bond with honesty. Bond with ambition. Bond with determination. Love what you do with all your heart and you will *bond* with success.

Enjoy your school year.

Step Forward

*E*very step backward is a lost gain. I recognize there are times of difficulty in life. Sometimes, seemingly insurmountable. The temptation to cave under, mistakenly viewed as an escape or relief, is not the answer. You will have added *regret* to yourself. Not all have been blessed with determination. I understand that. And it is why those who possess the capacity to perceiver should encourage and lead those who fail to recognize the potential seen in them by others. Find your fire and burn to a glow. Each time you succeed will addict you to the pleasure of challenge. Remember, don't step back. You can stop, evaluate, develop, and adapt accordingly. Now step forward.

Tony Amico

Backup

I'm recalling an incident that occurred several years back. A dump-truck loaded with macadam (blacktop around here), pulls up in front of my home. A man gets out, walks around back of my home where I'm standing, and asks if I need any pavement done super cheap as he has an extra load on his truck, and needs to get rid of it soon. I'm suspicious, but I do need a parking area paved in the rear. The price was dirt cheap, but he wanted cash, which I had that day. I directed him to the area in mind and inquired if he had help and equipment. He said he would momentarily if he could use my house phone. I cautiously allowed him inside. Shortly thereafter, an entire family arrived, a brother, perhaps brother-in-law, wives, children. A *distraction* group. I could see I put myself and my family at risk. The men proceeded to prepare the driveway, and I quietly directed my then wife, to make a call to someone special and explain the situation. Within minutes some friends of mine appeared and observed as all was carried out to plan. Good to have backup.

(True story)

Life's Concert

Life is like a never-ending concert. You have an entrance, some great music, happy songs, sad songs, a few that fall flat, some really spectacular moments, and an ending without an encore. And then there are those who continue to talk about it afterwards keeping the music of our life alive. Give your best performance today. You never know when the curtain falls.

Dark and Lonely Path

Sometimes we walk a dark and lonely path. Our feet barely visible in front of us, as we struggle through every step. The sun rises ever so slowly at times like these. I know. I've walked on such a path. But I tell you, just as sure as the day turns brighter every day, the dark path will lighten up and widen, as you raise your eyes from your feet and look further ahead. There may be a mountain of troubling thoughts and obstacles clearly in view. But rest assured, there's a valley of opportunity just over the next horizon. By the way, now that the day begins to brighten. Notice those who were walking with you in the dark. Some were behind you, fearful that you might fall behind. Some were alongside in case you needed a helping hand or word of encouragement. A few were steps ahead of you, but always looking back to see that you were on track and following their lead. You see, the dark and lonely path is a mindset. Your steps follow your heart. You may stumble. Might even fall down, but always look up and all around yourself. You have to choose to be alone. You are not.

Given

There are things you may never experience in life. No need to be specific. Regrets? Perhaps, don't dwell. You can only re-live in your mind. You have your life. The one you've been given to be grateful for. The life you've been given custody of. You have the responsibility to decorate it in a most creative manner. To do less is self-vandalism. Be proud to be among those who've enhanced not only their lives, but yours as well, by being a part of your life's experience. There is so much to look forward to if you stop to paint the bright picture in your mind. Leave the dark paintings behind.

Service

𝑊hen you grew up in my era, you were surrounded by veterans.

World War 2, Korea, Vietnam, and then later in life, Desert Storm. I am so grateful to all who served in any capacity. God bless you for your service.

Why

I remember the lean times very well. It's why today, I say there's always a way. You just have to be willing. One winter I was asked about building a small addition for a friend. I had to excavate 60 running feet of footer, 43" deep. After I cleared the snow, I dug by hand, alone. Poured the footer, mixed mud, humped and laid the block by myself. Why? I needed the money to pay bills, feed my family, and do what was necessary to survive. I look back at those times with fondness now. It taught me a valuable lesson. "Failure is for those who quit." I don't. Neither should anyone else who believes in themselves. It's not easy. But then anything worth achieving isn't easy. You must do what's necessary, so you'll appreciate what you've got. I laugh at myself now, when I reflect on this one of many such stories. And I laughed then when someone asked, "But why?"

Five-Year Plan

*I*n speaking with someone much younger than myself recently, I offered this career focused advise. You can't afford to spend more than five years in the wrong direction. And if you are willing to devote five motivated, focused, undistracted years to something you truly believe in doing, you'll either succeed or learn from the experience. If you can give up more than you take for five years, you have to come out ahead. Set your plan in motion. Put the blinders on. Don't waste time. Spend it productively. You can be so much more than you ever dreamed possible, if you push yourself and refuse to be distracted. The energy level you possess between the ages of 18 and 30 are the greatest you'll ever have. Just my thoughts before the sun rises.

Painting Life with Words of Encouragement

Wooden Box

*P*icture a wooden box. Old. A bit weathered, a few scratches here and there. But an attractive patina. Still intact. The hinge and clasp are secure. Within are held all that you are. Your memories kept lovingly in place. Between the folds of notes to self and others from time to time are the things you wish you said. And the ones you wish you'd never spoken. Take a moment. Close your eyes and imagine an expression on a face you wish you could touch once more. It's in the box now. Along with a thread from a child's sweater. And an old spoon you fed your memories with all these years. Ah yes, there's that photo of someone you haven't spoken to in a while. Why not? Hey, here's a token from a trip with someone special. And oh, a time you couldn't make it comes to mind. As you view, reminisce, long for, regret, laugh, cry...into the box. The inside lid now fully opened. There's a mirror. You are the box. Keep the lid open.

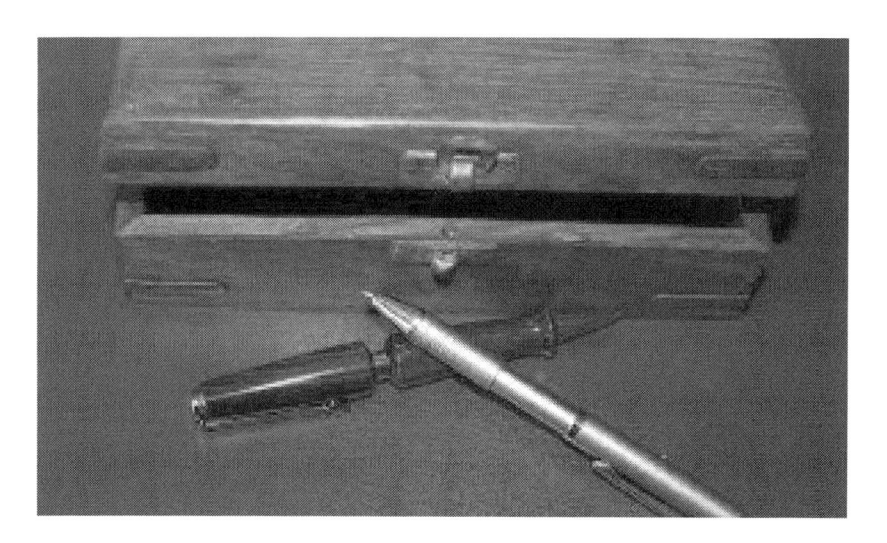

Lesson

A lesson I learned many years ago. Oh, I sometimes forget. But then I remember a desperate time when I thought there was nowhere to turn. But when it comes to the lowest point, there is someone to turn to. To turn over to. To look to. And wait for the relief from whatever you are plagued by. And then you recognize the familiarity of faith. It was never in my hands to begin with.

Our Thinking

I often touch on a reason to persevere. To push yourself. Don't settle, etc. Believe me when I tell you, the days I'm on my game, literally speaking, I've been thinking and talking inside. What do I need to hear? What have, or haven't I done already? What am I grateful for? Who has it far worse than me? And soon I'm thinking, *What can I say, do, pray for, talk to, reach out to, ask to forgive, offer to forgive?* Flawed as we all are, being honest with ourselves will translate to honesty with others. I feel the greatest success in life will come from being a successful human being. Don't give up. Give out. Don't raise your hands. Extend them. Don't step back. Step in. Talk really is cheap. Listening is invaluable.

Tony Amico

Puzzles

$\mathcal{A}$s time changes us, our influences, experiences, effects of work, health, friendships, etc. We reflect and ponder questions, *What I wish I did differently. What might have been.* But I believe in destiny. We are part of a grand puzzle. Each of us formed and shaped to fit in. Some of us are part of the background. Some are part of the main object meant to be focused on. Some are the edging holding it together. And, of course, there's an extra piece sometimes waiting to find a place to fit in. Well, those may be the ones held in the Creator's hand awhile. Perhaps intended for a different puzzle. I suppose the best place to be is, the piece being turned and moved from place to place getting close to the other shapes. And learning how to be a part of what we really don't want to see completed. My thoughts this morning at 4:30 am.

Painting Life with Words of Encouragement

$\mathcal{P}$icture for a moment, a puzzle. A puzzle depicting a grand painting. It has all the elements of something unique and spectacular. It is vibrant and moving. colorful and exhilarating. You think you have all the time in the world to find and place the pieces that will bring it all to life. And yet, you can't wait to see it materialize in front of your eyes. But somewhere along the way, the most precious piece of the puzzle is lost. Irretrievably lost. The picture will never be complete. Oh, there are areas to view, admire, and behold. Even to enjoy and to share. Yet, it cannot be completed, because that one piece, can't be retrieved. Can't be duplicated. Can't be substituted with anything else. And that, my dear friends and family, is what a life, altered by tragedy, looks like. And so, you gather the pieces often. You dismantle and reconstruct the puzzle. Knowing there is a piece missing. And you move in every other direction of the incomplete picture. Knowing what is missing. Feeling the void within always. You cannot fill in your own, but you can add yourself to someone else's painting. You can be the unexpected image in their puzzle. I hope I can be such a fragment as often as possible.

Open Door

Every now and then a door will open.
Sometimes just ajar.
Enough to alert you of an opportunity
Just waiting to be experienced.
Move closer.
View through the opening.
Grab hold of the door before it closes.
Step in and embrace the moment that may be just for you.

Empty or Full

Talent is great.

Skill is an asset.

Experience, certainly helpful.

Determination, necessary.

And having all of these qualities,

but lacking passion, desire, commitment,

 and humility,

you are nothing but a vessel.

An empty one at that.

Love what you do with all your heart.

Life's Meaning

Life is about beginnings and endings. Jobs, relationships, difficult times, and good times. All come to an end, for various reasons, beyond our capacity to control. Where we choose to remain in life will determine how we enjoy a new beginning or remain in *the end*. There is no life living in the end, of that which is no more. Remembering and reminiscing isn't the same as pining and longing to be in a place that no longer is. Eventually, we must move toward a beginning and leave behind the end. A brand-new day is upon us already. Begin it with the wonder of a child in your eyes. Take in every moment and enjoy sharing the experience of all that is new in today's life. See you all at sunrise.

Thread of Life

You only have to speak to someone, or recall someone who lost a loved one unexpectedly, to realize what a fine thread connects us from life to death. Don't take anyone's presence for granted. Don't take life for granted. All can and will change in an instant. We have an obligation to appreciate and to be appreciated by those whose lives we are privileged to impact. Do your *best* to be your best. You may be the one holding on to another's *thread of life*, today, tomorrow, the next five minutes.

Tony Amico

Encouragement

And so, we move forward. Not easy, but necessary. Sometimes we need reminders of a past, to deal with the present. Here's a story for you: I was in a local restaurant, sitting on the farthest side from the door. When I see a familiar face from a long time ago. A man whom I had one conversation with over 30 years ago. I was a despondent young boy, dealing with a breakup of my first serious relationship. My mom was worried about me. I'd grown quiet. A bit distant. She called a young priest from our parish to talk to me. He called me. Took me to lunch. And listened. I spoke of terrible thoughts, such as driving my car into a bridge wall. He offered his guidance away from such ideas. He encouraged me. Gave me a reason to desire living through adversity. Relying on my faith, I sent a drink to his table. Waited a few minutes and walked over to re-introduce myself to a man who'd forgotten my face and my story, from so long ago. I told him, in front of his friends, that he may be the reason why we are here in the same room having our conversation all these many years later. I, the boy barely out of his teens, and he, the young man fresh out of seminary, were once again in front of one another. I was now almost 60 and he was close to retiring from the priesthood. Like bookends to a small volume of storybooks. I reminded him of his purpose and value in my life. And I too was reminded of his effect on me with just a few words of support. Words of sincerity heal. And those who speak to your heart are sincere in the truest form. Now, I don't know what affect my words had on him. But I'm well aware of the affect his words had on me. Thank you, Father Pauselli for altering my course so many years ago.

Priceless

As you move forward through the days, months, years, and moments of your life, you will be loved, hurt, amused, betrayed, respected, and disrespected. There will be those who will mentor to you. And, of course, those you may wish to forget. Oh, the days of incredible joy. And sadly, the times of terrible despair. The moments you were caught off guard. The moments you expected. The exuberant celebrations. The quiet moments of reflection. The crying days. The laughing nights. This, in all its glorious, complicated splendor, is life. A gift having no equal. More than you deserve. Less than expected. An unimaginable journey into a familiar, yet unknown place. Live every moment like a carnival ride. Explore, absorb, rejoice, pause, run, and wallow. Most of all, appreciate life. It is truly *priceless* and irreversible in every way.

Faith Full

I've been dealt a few cards over the years that I'd rather not have had to play. Haven't we all. And from the outsider's perspective, I may be viewed in various manners. If I project any image of my character, I would hope my faith is at the forefront. There is no greater feeling, than knowing the worst things in life can be given over to One so much greater prepared to handle them, than I could ever be. All of life's trials and hurdles are a part of a character-building process. Flawed as we may be, admittedly so, we are accepted, loved, encouraged, and viewed as perfect in God's eyes. I have a hard time seeing myself as I'm told He sees me. I know I've given Him reason to cringe from time to time. Still, I'm aware. And will remain, regardless of circumstances, *faith-full*.

For the Young and Hungry

When you dream, dream big. Don't analyze your desires, just plan the course as best you can. You'll make directional changes along the way, but never change your focus. You'll find, when you are willing to step out, you'll encounter nay sayers. Ignore them? No! They are the fuel for your engine. Their negative opinions are to be taken in, burned in your determined engine. And expelled like exhaust. You may be introduced to something you may not have considered. Be open as long as it fits with your spirit. Remember, you have to love what you do to be good at it. In time, you may find you aren't getting as far as you expected. Don't get discouraged. This is *your* plan you are building on. Continue improving yourself. It's a lifelong commitment. You cannot, nor should you, concede to failure. Adjust, adapt and overcome. Look at yourself in the mirror every day. Make sure you turn away looking more confident every time. People can see confidence. Confident people can spot weakness. You need to understand why this is so essential to your success. And finally, never finish the game. If you are a believer, your faith will carry you through the dark times. If I were to live my life over, the only thing I'd do differently, is take greater risks. Much greater. Scarier risks. What's the worst that could happen? You're still here. You're still alive. You have an opportunity to learn from a mistake, which can only prepare you for success. Very important, be a successful human being. Play fair. Don't cheat. Your character is your reputation. Compel those you encounter, to say good things about you. Plan on making those who matter most, feel good about being in your circle. And for those who don't get it, they are insignificant to you. Sorry. Winners hang with winners. Be one. God bless.

Be Yourself

Say what's on your mind.

    Some will be amused.

        Some may be offended.

            Some may be inspired or moved.

        But be straight forward and most of all be yourself.

    Honesty should be respected, regardless of opinion.

At least it's how I see it.

Naivety

I've read so many posts lately. Some happy, some sad. Tragedies, difficulties, celebrations, mourning's. Yes, it is life. As it comes. Not always as expected or wished. My heart feels heavy tonight as I reflect on my thoughts. And so, I refocus. The night is calm and warm. The sun still in the sky on this second day of another glorious summer. I saw the faces of innocent children today. They were naive and full of wonder. Oblivious to the trials of adulthood. We had our time of childhood too. But now, our responsibility, it would seem to me, is to keep them naive as long as possible. And hopefully, one day, they will be better adults than their teachers. Well, at least, I hope so.

Tony Amico

Blessed

I woke up at 4:00 am. Stood on my own two feet. I can breathe unassisted. Walk, see, hear, and think clearly. There are those who would be glad to do *one* of those. I have it all. I'm a blessed man. Today I'm thinking of those who are blessed differently than me. Who appreciate more with less. Those who accept. Give thanks. And forge onward, regardless. God bless them.

Nostalgia

I was walking down the street of nostalgia just a short time ago. I stepped off the curb and as I looked up a dead end block I noticed many were alive. Oh, the faces I saw. Too many to mention. I'm sure you understand, but it was so much more than that. There were voices I recalled. And childhood birthday parties in the summer sun. Hey, there's a hose fight going on. Now what happened to the pavement, the street turned back to dirt. Well that looks like fun. My goodness, everybody has a garden. I looked down at my feet, I was wearing PF Flyers, guess I could run faster and jump higher now. Not too many cars around, good thing, because they're so damn big. As I reached the end of the block, the sounds of the old neighborhood was alive and well in my ears. I think I heard my name called home for supper. But they're getting ready to play Kick the Can. I turned around to run home and all went silent. The street turned back to pavement. And everyone was gone. And what about... Oh, I'm wearing work shoes. Guess I shouldn't have turned around.

Storm Clouds

When you feel the dark clouds moving in, take it. Absorb it. Deal with it. And anticipate the brighter day to follow. You will emerge. Perhaps wounded. But stronger. By the way, grab the *faith* umbrella.

Victor

There's perpetual motion in the daily grind.
 Defeat always being a state of mind.

No matter what obstacle or cause for dismay,
 A pause in your stride is but a delay.

Strategic maneuvers, negotiating words,
 Sidesteps and hurdles as each one occurs.

Bring it to your Maker and heed what is said,
Then relinquish the problem and consider it dead.

Humility, virtuous as often said,
 Couple with your Savior the advisory dreads.

So, sample the pitfalls learn from mistakes,
 Savor the flavor of victory's taste.

Welcome the trials and laborious toil,
 And you'll be a victor of the *ultimate* spoil.

Tony Amico

Therapy in Iron

*I*t was part promise, part self-indulgence. A source of laughter and a cause for smile. It was a reason to be alone and yet gave me company. Though Michel was not there, he was with me all the time. I spent seven months with this piece of iron; sanding, dismantling, rebuilding, enjoying the challenge, the frustration, churning out the time, the effort, and the finances. Talking to myself, whistling, humming, talking to my son, and audibly mimicking his responses to my questions.

Bolt by bolt, fender by fender, my door, his door, the wheels and tires, the details, the license plates, Michel's picture...and that first ride, seemingly alone, I drove with my son's sprit in the passenger seat. Part of me was restored also.

So, for 13 years, each and every time I drive this truck, I remember all it took was my time. But it gave me back so much in return, only my smile can reveal.

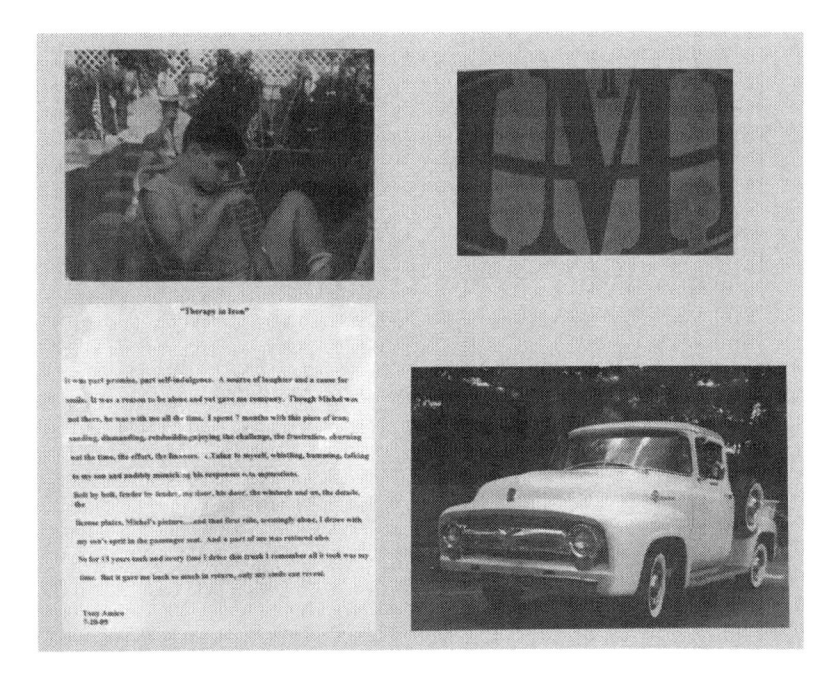

Tragic

The greatest tragedy in life is experienced by the unbeliever.

They must face adversity alone.

When the family and friends disband, they are truly alone.

There's a line in a song," Who can I turn to, if you turn away…" It's meant to refer to a lover, but in practical sense, it can be interpreted to those who think they have nowhere to turn.

No matter how bleak the moment, in the darkest of hours – facing seemingly insurmountable challenges or tragedies--we are *never* alone.

In Jesus' words, "I will *never* leave you or forsake you."

Tony Amico

Losses and Gains

1976, I'm 18-years-old. I'm facing a future of hard labor (I didn't know it then, thought I was going to be a millionaire). The American Freedom Train was docked at the Lackawanna Station. I can almost hear her puffing steam. My eyes brightly full of wonder, my hair black, and not an ache or a pain to distract me. In two years, I would be a father. In five years, I'd be a businessman and a homeowner. Arlo Guthrie is singing The City of New Orleans. The years to follow are moving quicker than I expected. I'm determined and ambitious, but blind to the preciousness of life. One day, that would change in an instant. Like a slap in the face. And an unending sting of reality. The years move quicker still. But time moves slowly, if that makes any sense. I am humbled by life's lessons and live in a perpetual world of optimism. No matter the trials of life, your losses or gains are one in the same. There is no perfect life, there is only life. And we are an example to the young, bright eyed, stars in their eyes generation to follow. They should know there is so much to live for, to laugh about, to explore fearlessly. Ride their dreams like horses full of fire, but tell them, like we were told, "It's a quick ride on the Merry-Go-Round, and I'll ride it ever smiling."

A Horse Called Life

I'm riding a horse called, Life.

He bears my weight like a feather,
sometimes carrying me in the rain of tears.
Always at the ready,
as we ran through the early years.

Life is a spirited fellow,
a pounding heart a determined stride.
Yet humble enough to reign in my pride.

He's big and white like a new fallen snow.
His eyes are piercing like a full moon aglow.

I grasp his mane in my hand
as he gathers ground and speed.
How blessed am I to ride this marvelous steed?

Life slows at times to allow me to gather,
The times and ideas I thought didn't matter.

Dismount, I think *not*.
Life slows and turns but never will he stop.

And when my ride is over
he'll cast me from his back,
So, we both will walk together
where there are no tears and nothing more to lack.

Tony Amico

Painting Life with Words of Encouragement

Family

Tony Amico

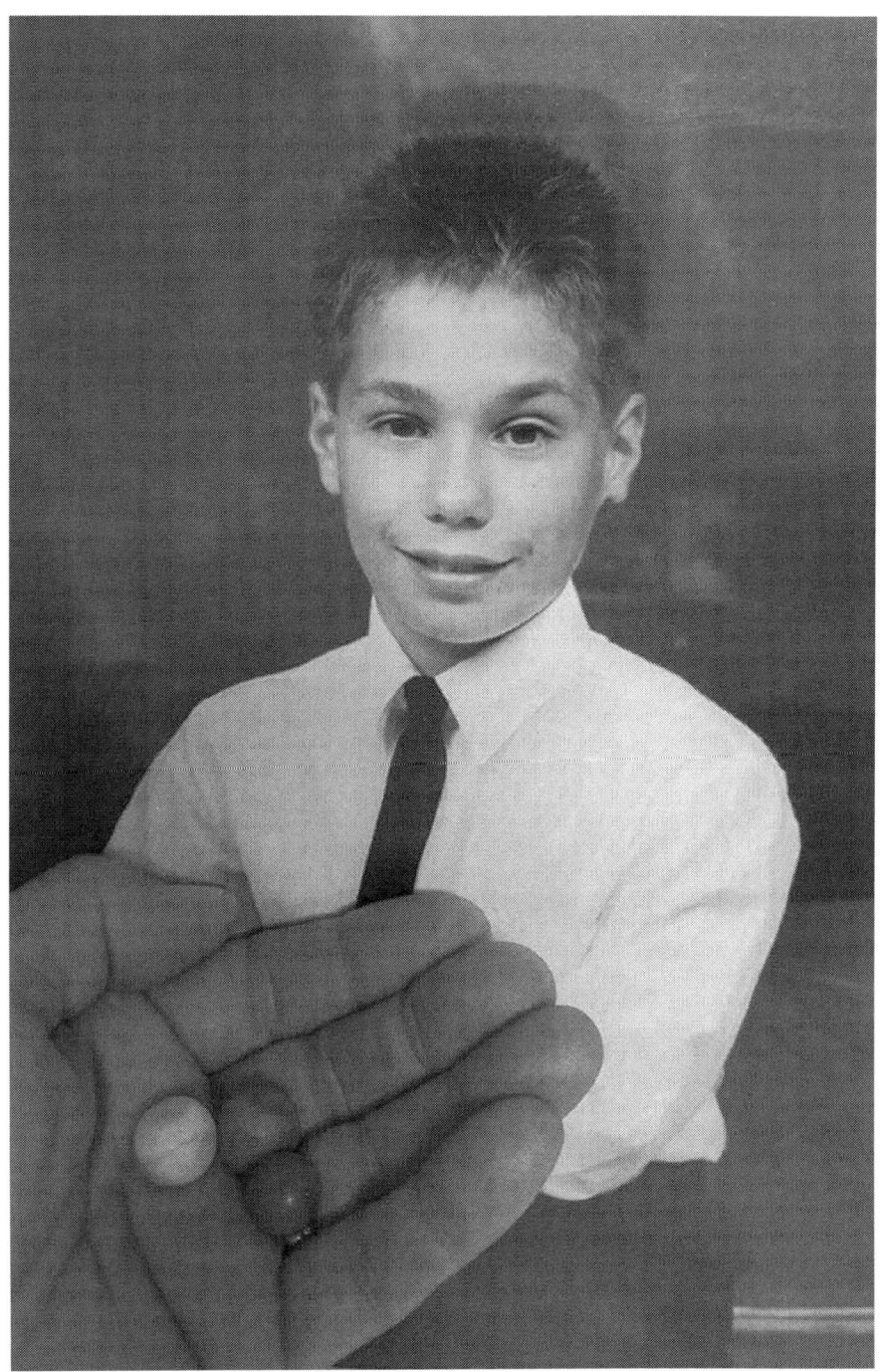

Michelangelo Amico 9/18/1978 – 8/25/1993

Painting Life with Words of Encouragement

Marbles

Tomorrow the sun will rise, much as it did on August 25, 1993. It was a "Steel Blue Sky" as I recall. My Son, Michel would spend our last day together. Little did I realize it then. I certainly would have altered the course of events. We had breakfast that morning at "The Mid Valley Diner" (No longer exists), Michel claimed they made the best omelets. From there we traveled to South Scranton. We were preparing for a cellar entrance way. Excavating by hand. It was there he gave me the last things that would ever pass between our hands. 3 marbles. (I still have them) As we dug, the first of which was light blue. He tossed it to me; I missed his catch but picked it up and placed it in my pocket. The second one he dug up (a bit darker in color, but also blue) and threw my way, I caught. And placed it in my pocket. And the third of which was much smaller than the other two and a much deeper blue, I caught also. And placed in my pocket. I remember the day as if it were a video playing over and over again in my mind. And every August 25th I will relive every moment as it plays out. But the marbles will always be a significant part. You see at the end of the day after losing my Son, being devastated and exhausted, in the wee hours of the morning, still in shock, I suppose.... I recall emptying my pockets and finding those now oh so special marbles. Realizing what was in my hand, they now represent a significant part of him and I. The first marble, the one I missed, represents the part of his life I missed, when I wasn't paying attention and failed him as a Father. The second marble, darker in color. The one I caught, is the part of him I never lost sight of. And continue to hold onto. And then there's the third and last of the marbles, small, dark blue. It represents, what's left of me without him. And although there is such a great and precious piece of my life missing; and regardless of the many tears I've shed, on so many August 25th's, I recognize, that the sky will be "Steel Blue" again. I have many reasons to laugh and smile. I have the memories that only God and Michel could have given me. And my faith is as strong as it has ever been. Encouraging me to encourage others. To do my best. To leave a "Respectable mark" on this earth. If for no other reason, then to honor my 'Michel'. And tomorrow, the marbles will be in my pocket. They are the most valuable of my material possessions. They are "Priceless" in any sense. So, if you happen to see me in your travels on that day, ask me if "I have all my Marbles". And I'll show that I do indeed.

Till we meet again, my boy, I love you with all my heart, deep to my very soul. Your Father.

Tony Amico

The Footprints

My mantra has always been to find the good in the bad. Sometimes it's a very difficult search. How to end a sad story on a high note is most difficult. My Michel passed on a Wednesday, August 25th, 1993. It was during a hot dry spell of summer.

The viewing, the funeral and the following days are a bit of a blur to me. Even now, there are gaps in my recollection of those days. But one memory will forever haunt me even though I have become accustomed to telling the story.

The Monday following the funeral, I returned to work accompanied by two of my closest friends, John Perry and George Mallas. They are among several of my friends who saw to my state of mind in the difficult times.

Michel and I were in the middle of a stone patio project on the last day of his life. It was on this last day when I complimented him on what a fine example of a man I could see him developing into. He was toned and tan, an ambitious boy of fourteen, handsome, and popular.

Anyway, on this fateful day as I entered the jobsite, I was greeted by his footprints still clearly visible in the sand. I froze, dead in my tracks, realizing these were among his last footsteps on this earth. I had all I could do to contain my tears and move in any direction that might erase this last trace of his existence in this world. But life must move in a forward direction, otherwise it isn't life.

I moved through the day. My dear friends at my side. Each footstep I took, erasing those of my only child. Each stone I set entombed his youthful span of just under fifteen years.

Eventually the job was done, the patio completed, my son's steps once recorded, now erased. And the next steps taken, would be those of my own as I stepped into this world without Michel to call me Pa or Dad. But step forward I did, and still do, with him in my heart, my mind, and in my soul. He is within my spirit and is now a part of my steps in the sands of life.

Painting Life with Words of Encouragement

Once a Dad

On a warm sunny day, you entered the world and I was suddenly Dad.
And dream, how I dreamed of a lifetime in store,
Not knowing how little you had.
But grateful am I and so fortunate too,
For the blessing of life and a son that was you.
The first steps you took, my thumbs in your hands,
All memories vivid as the time your life spans.
The first words you spoke I may not recall,
But calling me Dad is what I miss most of all.
So full my life was, and you nourished my pride,
But I took it for granted as you walked by my side.
Day after day, year after year…
Wouldn't you always be ever so near?
Those who stepped out of our lives, some who left this earth.
These are the realities of life, since the day of our birth.
Time marches on, changes to come,
I tried my best to be a good father to you, my one and only son.
My Michel, my Michel, I just couldn't see,
Where destiny was leading, my dreams were not to be.
And so, I walk through this life holding memories deep inside,
Sometimes I see your smile and my walk turns to a stride.
Even though I cannot touch you or run my fingers through your hair,
I can close my eyes and wander in my dreams, you're always there.
So, when my time is over, when my walk is finally done,
I'll step into the splendor with you, my loving son.

Tony Amico

Book of Faces

*T*here's a book of faces that I leaf through often. Some of the pages are worn more than others from frequent viewing. The book is a one copy edition. Although, many other volumes share similar images of the same individuals. The expressions on the faces are familiar to me. They make me laugh and cry. I hesitate to turn certain pages sometimes. Not because I don't want to see them. But rather because I do. Oh, I want so much to pull them from that book of faces so dear to me, and always increasing in size. And yes, one day my face will grace the page of someone else's book. Not mine though. On that day my book of faces will have been viewed for the last time. I urge you all to take your own book to heart. It may not be a best seller. But it's limited and priceless. God bless us all.

Pets

Not everyone is an animal lover. I get that. I know those who aren't. For whatever reason that may be. And it doesn't make them bad, less, or indifferent. But for those of us who know and understand what it is to have the love of a pet. To give love to a pet. To feel compassion, dependency, forgiveness, admiration, companionship, friendship, and unconditional love from one who has never spoken a word to you. We could only hope to be influenced by them so completely that we recognize our flaws because of their Unspoken words. I, for one of many, am truly blessed to have the treasured relationships that I've had in my life with God's creatures.

Tony Amico

Great Danes

There have been Great Danes in my life for many years. Other breeds as well, but the Danes hold a special bond with me. As a child, it was a Dane who released me from a fear of dogs and recreated a boy who loved them. As an adult, they played an important role in my own son, Michel's life. I saw to it he'd never have a fear being raised as an infant with them. There was a span of years without one. Circumstances in my life created an unreceptive atmosphere for a dog. And then I found my wife, Valerie. After sharing the memories of the times in my son's and my life, (Michel passed in 1993) it was apparent that the Danes were a living part of my history. Having them in my life now, allows me to hold onto all those years before in an almost current sense. I hope this makes sense to most. I'm able to hug my life of years through them. I look into the eyes of time. There have been two in recent years. Nero, who showed Val why Danes are different. We lost him in 2011. And Mason, who encompassed the very best qualities of this magnificent breed. We lost him on July 4, 2017 has opened an awful wound in our hearts. But in time, it will heal. Although, leaving a loving scar. Will there be another? I don't know. I hope so. But the Danes will always be a part of this incredible journey of life. They are not a dog to me.

Coal

When still in grade school, my dad and my Uncle Jimmie, being the two oldest boys, would be awakened by my Grandfather Salvatore, at 4:00 am to follow him to the mines before his shift began. Walking with their wagons in tow to be filled with chunks of coal. Grandpa would stay at the mine for work and send the boys home in the dark with their payload. They would wash up for school and afterwards crack the coal with hammers to make ready for the heatrola (coal stove). They would have it done before their father returned home from the mine. Kids have it tough today. Really?

One of my Dad's stories.

Tony Amico

Grandpa

My Grandpa Mike was a quiet man. Strong, good looking, but weathered from life's experiences. My memories are mostly visual. He never said much and when he did, it was in Italian. I remember his smile, his laugh and that vise like grip when he'd reach for my arm when I was a child. He'd pull me in and hug a part of himself he probably never dreamed he'd see. I can almost smell the lingering pipe smoke in the kitchen of so long ago. Thinking back, I can recall how his eyes revealed the wounded soul that was left after losing my Grandma Ida. Her passing swept him up with her. Never to be the same again. These were my mom's parents. I see their mark on her every day. In the quiet of this morning, I can recall Grandpa Michel Delfino making coffee and toast for me and smiling just because I was there. How special a time, and yet so simple.

Grandpa Mike Delfino

Painting Life with Words of Encouragement

Grandmother

So, on this, the anniversary of my grandmother's birth (the 17th), Josephine Amico, and the day before my son, Michelangelo's, I imagine taking a seat in an old woven lawn chair in back of my grandmother's house. It's a cool September day with a bright warm sun. Like so many others, at this time of year. And exactly like one on a particular September day 39 years ago, I feel my grandmother's presence behind me. Her warm embrace around my shoulders. I lean back into her and tell her a tale, "Like many others, Grandma, you included, I've buried a child. I look to my left hand and there is the memory of exuberance and a joyful birth of my only child. The memories of his childhood. The pictures of him smiling, racing through my thoughts. And in my right hand, a tragic end. Just shy of 15 years on this Earth. A memory burning a hole in my heart and probably aging me."

My grandmother reaches down, grasps both my arms, crosses them over my chest, and whispers in her sweet, sweet voice, "All is a ina you heart now. You hold asa I'ma hold you from a place we all gonna be, one bright sunny day, just a lika this. Goda bless."

Grandma Amico

I was blessed to have met all my grandparents in my lifetime. Although, because I was young when most of them passed, my recollection of them is mostly from the stories passed on to me from other family members. Fortunately, my Grandma Amico was with me into my thirties. She lived downstairs from us. And so, I had daily contact. Numerous sit-downs over coffee. And the greatest memories of being loved by her. I can recall the sound of her voice. The way she laughed. The touch of her hand on mine. And that wonderful soft cheek that I kissed every day, as I passed through her kitchen. She is so much a part of who I am today. As are many, for various reasons. But Grandma stands alone, rightly so, as she comes to mind today. She's in my heart always. She instilled so much that her memory is alive with her very spirit surrounding me, whenever I recall her. I close my eyes and the door opens. There she is, in the kitchen. I take in the aroma of her coffee. Or I walk into the parlor, she's sitting crocheting, watching a soap opera. Most of all, were the life lessons she bestowed upon me. Her stories, which are mine because of her sacrifice. And now, I leave her as she remains always, within my being. I embrace her, kiss her, and feel her warm loving hands caress my face as we part.

Painting Life with Words of Encouragement

Grandma Josephine Amico

This is a real time picture of Grandma Amico's Kitchen taken from a video I made of her home years after she passed and before a tenant moved in.

Tony Amico

Grandma's Hugs

$\mathcal{A}$ blanket once owned by my Grandma Delfino, my maternal grandmother, repaired by my Grandma Amico, my paternal grandmother, given to me by my sweet cousin, Michele Dutko. It's like being hugged by both grandmas at once. Thank you, Michele.

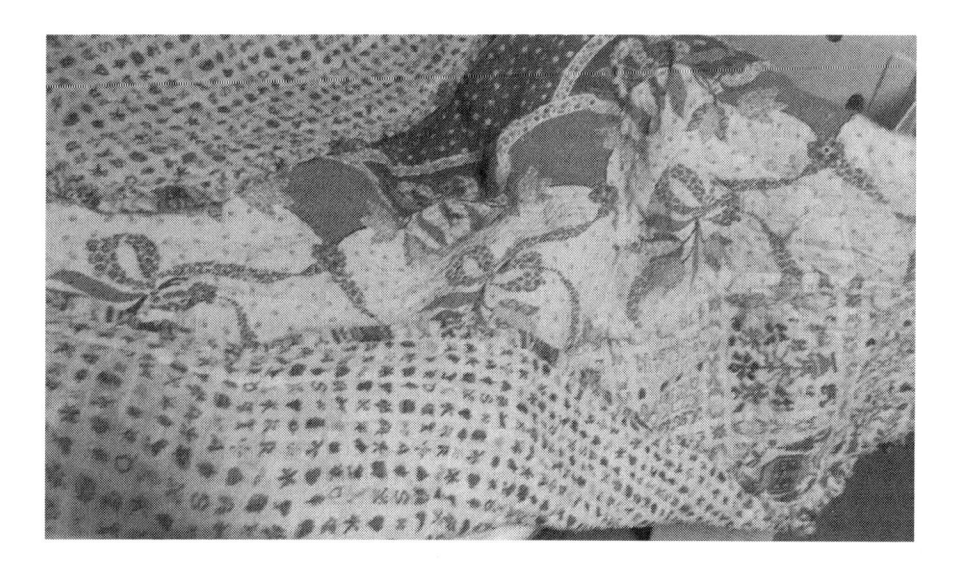

Painting Life with Words of Encouragement

Cousin

As a child, one of my fondest memories is the Saturday fishing days with my cousin, Chico (Vince Delfino). He was the first to buy and place a fishing pole in my hand and spend countless hours with me, teaching me the do's and don'ts of the craft. We literally fished from the break of dawn to dusk. Laughed most of the day. Hit every river, creek, stream, lake in an area covering an incredible number of miles. We fished in rain and cold, caught in open water in lightning storms, and endless sunny days. Sadly, as an adult this was a leisure pleasure my business took away from me. But I have the fondest memories of that special time of my youth. It was wonderful having a cousin eight years my senior to bond with, then and now.

Tony Amico

Painting Life with Words of Encouragement

Personal

Once Again

*I*f only to step into the shoes of the boy who still lives within me.

To absorb the innocence of naivety just for little while. To have all that is no longer, as if it was never lost or passed. Just a few minutes of wonderment under a star lit sky. When the clarity of life was obscured by laughter. When all that I held was also what held me. When my imagination wasn't derailed by reality. Ok, I've stepped there. I've listened, and I've seen. And I've taken in just enough to imagine the tomorrow to come. A piece of yesterday in my heart to get me along. And to share a bit more of myself with anyone it may interest.

Painting Life with Words of Encouragement

These Hands

These are the hands that were held by Mom for the first time, as she counted each finger one by one.

These are the hands my dad grasped looking into the eyes of his son.

These are the hands that were taught to pray, as they have ever since and still do today.

These are the hands that held tightly my sister's arms closely. Time has not changed the hold she still has on me.

These are the hands that played catch with my brother, who watched out for me then and still does as no other.

These are the hands that learned to read and write, and one day held the book that led me to the light.

These are the hands that held my son for the first time, the same hands that held him for the last time.

These are the hands that held my face full of tears. They are also the ones that toiled through the years.

These are the hands that took my soul mate to be my bride. These are the hands my caress will never hide.

These are the hands that my friends have come to know, a bond formed once and never to grow old.

These are the hands that turned the pages of my days. And wiped tears away from others, as sorrow blurred their gaze.

These are the hands that seal the promise of my word, in volumes never spoken but always to be heard.

These are the hands that will weather and one day may not work as well. But they will continue trying until the toll of the bell.

One day these hands will be placed one over the other, rest assured, I'll grasp the hand of One far greater than any other.

Tony Amico

Anapra

*I*n 1997 I went on a mission trip to Mexico, along with a few close friends. We went there to lay block on an orphanage under construction. Among the many rewarding experiences of that time, was a day that truly stands out. We took a break from our daily work to venture into a makeshift village named, Anapra, just south of the border. So close, in fact, that the U.S. flag was clearly visible from where we stood. The homes were made of pallets, scrap lumber, or salvaged building supplies. The electricity was pirated from utility poles with extension cords, the likes of which I'd never seen. We smuggled in duffle bags filled with standards, tooth paste, brushes, combs, children's clothes, candies, some small toys, etc. As we entered the village the children began to converge on our vehicle, knowing from experience what we were there for. I remember exiting the van with the duffle bag and literally being taken to the ground by a swarm of children. I laughed as I made it back to my feet to distribute what their wanting eyes longed for. I'll never forget the looks on their faces. The excitement in their eyes. For items always available to children just a short distance away. And then there was this little boy, who took the prepared bags I was handing out and first handed each one to those who were smaller than him. Taking his last. When I had emptied the bag, I reached in my pockets and held out my hands full of change as they picked it clean, like hungry birds. I remember the empty feeling I had when I had no more to give. And I experienced an emotion I'd never encountered. At that moment, the world was gray. And I was privileged to be in that moment. I was the one receiving as much or more than those I gave to.

True story

The Baby

Being the youngest of three, my sister Joann, the oldest, with brother Sam in the middle, I knew what it was like to be the *baby*. My parents gave me a bit more. I got away with more. My sister and brother played a large part in raising me. We're seven years apart. It was like having two moms and two dads. But when I grew to an age of recognition and appreciation, I could see just how blessed I was, and still am, to have the bond that made us a part of each other. We are so much more than flesh and blood. And it's a time such as this, that I find them deep within my heart. Where they have always been. And always will be. It's good to be the baby. Especially now at 60-years-old.

Grandma Delfino and me, the 'baby'

Tony Amico

Speeding

Here's another true story.

I was working in the Poconos from 1979 to 1980. I had bought an old unmarked Plymouth cruiser. Times were tough, but I was working hard. Coming home from work, driving down 380 toward Dunmore, and I have the speedometer buried. I catch a glimpse of a State Trooper with the radar gun pointed right at me as I crossed the Route 84 entrance. So, I put the gas pedal right to the floor thinking I could make the Tigue Street exit before he could catch up. Got caught behind a couple of 18-wheelers. Had to slow up a bit. And here he comes. Had to pull over. By this time, he's alongside me and pointing to the shoulder. He's not happy. I complied. The Trooper gets out and approaches my window.

"Do you have any idea how fast you were going?"

I responded, "I guess 100."

"96.5 mph. Let me have your license and registration."

I hand him what I have.

He checks it out and comes back furious now. This registration is for another car (Cadillac), your name, wrong car. The inspection expired six months ago. You altered your driver's license."

I had erased the seventh month, made it the first, so I could get served.

He ripped it up right in front of me. "And by the way, why were you going so fast?"

I answered, "I can't wait to get home to see my son."

He stopped dead in his tracks. "You're taking the day off tomorrow, young man. You're going to get this car legal and in order. You are going to report your license lost and file an Affidavit at the magistrate. At 3:00 pm tomorrow, I'll be in my office at Troop R, Dunmore waiting for you to produce the proper documentation. You'll come there with your son. If you don't, I'll have you arrested, not fined. Now slow down so your boy still has a father."

"Yes sir, I will." And I complied accordingly.

Sewers

Many years ago, I was preparing a rather naive worker (who's since become my friend) for a job we were about to do in a residential basement. (A sewer repair, blocked, etc.) I told him we were repairing a water line. (He's a bit squeamish). I also asked him to be on his best behavior because this was a very special client, highly educated and a retired professor holding a multitude of degrees and highly regarded locally. (In reality, I'm not sure he finished grade school). When we arrived at the estate (a dilapidated eyesore ripe for the wrecking ball.) I explained it was on the National Historic register. Then came the meeting. The "professor" came to the door, his hair in disarray, a 3-day beard shadow, a dingy t-shirt stained with last night's or several nights supper, a pair of suspenders holding up a pair of pants long past wearable service.

I whispered, "He's a bit eccentric, shh."

And then he spoke, leaving no doubt of his lack of civil refinement. At this point I got the "what the hell" look. It was the conversation of the day between us. And God bless this gentleman, he had no idea how he kept us smiling while digging up a plugged sewer line.

Tony Amico

The Funeral

A true Twilight Zone story,

A few years back, I went to a funeral service for someone I knew quite well. I glanced at the obituaries in the morning and made my way to the church. When I arrived, I was surprised to see such a sparse turnout. The hearse was parked outside the church and the funeral director was standing, as if waiting for the mourners. I thought it a bit strange when I approached and was asked if I wouldn't mind helping carry the body inside the church entrance. I responded without hesitation, "Why, I'd be honored." I grasped hold and climbed the steps with the other pallbearers, who I didn't recognize. Once inside, we positioned the coffin for viewing. Imagine the look on my face when they opened the casket and I gazed upon a face totally unfamiliar to me. I remember I almost blurted out, "Who the hell is that?" Quietly I stepped back, made my way to the door and drove away to the right church. Where the familiar faces were.

Painting Life with Words of Encouragement

Masonry by the Book

38 years ago, I made the brazen decision to enter the masonry field. I had no experience. Just a book on masonry, a desire to be successful, and the ambition God gave me. One day, I was forming a sidewalk, steps, etc. From time to time I had to refer to the book I had hidden in my pickup. The woman I was working for came out to compliment me on my forming process. She said she had a book inside her home. Said my forms were exactly as described. Then she brought out the book. Same one I had in the truck.

True story.

Tony Amico

Awards Night Speech

*I*n spite of the trials I, like anyone else have endured while living life, I've always been aware of the many blessings I've been exposed to. I must admit, I'm glad many of the teachers I had in High school are no longer here to see me, this unlikeliest one to impart wisdom, speaking to you tonight. I find it funny, myself. I count among my blessings, the many mentors who've shaped the character I've become. Some of you, might like to know who to blame. And long before I even knew what mentor meant, I encountered my first while in the first grade. You see, in those days of neighborhood schools the Art teacher would visit the schools to give a class once a week. That was when I met Jane Brier. She singled me out one day to praise me for an alligator I had shaped from clay, and marched me to every class in the building to show it off. It was the beginning of a bond that continued through my High school years and remains in my heart to this day. One day she took me aside as I was approaching my senior year, she explained what she saw in me through the years. (I thought I was the one studying her.) She described what set Artistic people apart, so that I could better understand her and myself. She said, "Tony, you see the world differently, you always have, and you always will. Your interpretation of colors and shapes will be as those viewed most creatively. You'll develop a certain mannerism in the way you speak, dress, write, and an appreciation for all the arts in a uniquely defined perception." And then she told me that I was, in her opinion, an Artist. Now, I tell this story, not to draw attention or praise to myself, but to her, for being so generous to me in her teaching, in her encouragement, and her guidance. I felt her hand in my life as if I was so much more than just her student. It was almost as if she was an extension of my parents. As one who was once a parent, I'd like to offer some words I wish I could be speaking to my son, Michel, but am honored and humbled to have your attention for just a bit longer. You see, it was here in this building that I, as a 14-year-old, was day dreaming during Art History class. I saw a day when I would have a son named Michelangelo. And 14 years after his birth, I would lose him. Had he lived to see a night such as this, here's what I might have shared with him:

Your parents have memories of your first steps. That day when you let go of your father's thumbs and stepped towards your mother's arms. One, two, three, yay...and they clapped and praised your accomplishment. You certainly don't remember how your heart must have been racing; the anticipation of what was coming next. The fear of falling, and the smile from ear to ear as you arrived safely to that loving embrace. Through the years, you've made many steps, too many to count now, and there'll be many more to follow as you travel life's path. Tonight, I hope you are focused on the next steps to come. Tomorrow, I hope you have the confidence to let loose of the thumbs as you did, not so long ago as a child. Oh, you may falter now and then, perhaps fall flat on your face, but the memory of every time you succeeded and the thrill of another accomplishment, should prepare you to take yet another step. Sometimes it's good to stop, turn around and look back. Just don't *step* back! Don't dwell on where you were, step where you've never been, and look past where you are. Focus on where you want to be. Your parents knew when to release you from their thumbs. They knew you would be all right then. And surely, they know now after watching you take so many steps. Now it's time to take bigger steps. Even risking steps into the dreams you have for yourself. Remember, short steps cover less ground in greater time. Big steps cover more ground in less time! One day, you will count your steps again, much as you did as a child, but by that time, you will have known if you took big enough steps to realize your dreams, as well as the dreams your parents hope for you to achieve, as you move along life's path. It's my pleasure to award tonight's scholarship in my son Michelangelo's name, to Ryan C.

Tony Amico

Kindergarten

As a 5-year-old, I hated Kindergarten. It was my only year in Catholic school. Sister Emma left a lasting impression, not a good one. I'd watch as some of the other children would cry and carry on, banging on the locked door. I was a schemer. My sister would walk me to school, or my godfather, Louie Viola would drive me there. As soon as they left my sight...I was gone. Half a block away was Grandma Amico's house. There I was greeted with love. Spoke to in Italian. Helped bake bread. Learned how to tend for and sometimes kill a chicken. (Grandma always said a little prayer before strangling.) I'd get to sit in on the Widow's card game once a week. Great cookies and Italian coffee. Grandma never scolded me much and when she did, I wasn't frightened like with Sister Emma. My grandma would tell me stories of her childhood in Italy. Wonderful stories of a place so far away and yet so closely dear to her heart. So, of the 180 school days, of which I may have attended half, the best Kindergarten was at Grandma's house.

"Antonio, wadda you do here?"

"I come to be with you, Grandma."

"No a school for you, ha?"

"No, Grandma, I don't like it there."

"Ok, you be good a boy, help Grandma do soma ting."

"Ok. Could I have some French toast first?"

"Ma sure, *aspetta*, wate a I git a apron."

Painting Life with Words of Encouragement

Tony Amico

Painting Life with Words of Encouragement

Letters

Tony Amico

A Birthday Note to My Wife

"My wife, Valerie, of 14 years is now 65. I really don't need anyone being patronizing by complimenting her or me for her youthful appearance.

It is strikingly apparent, to anyone who looks at her, that age will always be chasing her, and she will always be many steps ahead. Time will catch up to us all eventually, but God has given her an unusual blessing. She will remain somewhat childlike and yet youthfully sexy.

Valerie Amico

Tim

I want you to know something about the truck you purchased from me. During the summer of 1993, my son, Michel and I had many discussions, as we always did. Two of the topics which we spoke of most frequently, centered around my up-coming power lifting completion, and the possibility of restoring an old truck together that we would complete in time for his graduation in 1997.

Michel took his own life in August of 1993 at the age of 14.

As God allowed me to emerge from my despair, I found some comfort in completing some of the things he and I spoke of. In 1994, I competed in the North American Natural Power Lifting Competition and won 1st place in my weight class. A bittersweet win, knowing it would have pleased my son. I would have loved to hand that trophy off to him for his encouragement.

The late summer of 1996 brought the '56 Ford F100 into my plans and proved to be a challenge and an undertaking I can recall, as if it were a dream, involving another character called, Tony, like it wasn't me.

Tony Amico

Ida and Mike

*T*ime races onward erratically and meaningless
Lest we forget the gift of memory
A fortune of moments frozen in time
Some tormenting, while others so pleasantly painful
Oh...the memories of you
A child running in fear of a reprimand
I rush to the security of your arms
A fortress and yet soft surrounded
By the angelic aura of your loving eyes.
Oh...the memories of you
A windswept night in December
Your face so cold and yet so warm
I thank God for preserving these few memories
Of your forever lasting embrace
My tiny hand secure in your palm
The taste of your food, the rocking chair
So full of life that it died with you
Oh...the memories of you
And you...how you taunted though ever so gently
Pulling at her apron strings
The devilishness in your eyes
Was but a veil hiding the male counterpart
Of her loving intent
Oh...the memories of you
And when life's passing erased her tender existence
The death of your personality
Would painfully remind us of your loss
A void so vast and endless
A tie of black, the statues in her honor
And empty gaze so hopeful and so fruitless
Oh...the memories of you
The great artist will proceed with painting
Although, I'm sure he exhausted his ability
When he painted your faces
And when the first stroke of his brush
Meets with the last
I am confidently assured we will be as before
                         Forever embedded, Tony

Painting Life with Words of Encouragement

Ida and Mike

Tony Amico

Painting Life with Words of Encouragement

Short Stories

Tony Amico

Painting Life with Words of Encouragement

Joe, from Forty Fort

There's this guy named Joe. He's from a town named Forty Fort, Pennsylvania. Joe's father was a plumber and the town dentist, now retired and disabled, he resides in a nursing home. He believes he was hired as the resident dentist (they have to keep hiding his pliers).

Joe's mom, Merna, age 86 thinks she's 29-years-old, thinks she's a stripper, lives at home with Joe, his wife of two years, Hilda, she's from Austria, and Joe's mom's older brother, Steve.

The strange thing about Steve's sister, Joe's mom is she seems perfectly normal most of the time. But, every time she hears the song, *Tie a Yellow Ribbon* she starts stripping. Unfortunately, the song plays most often in elevators and grocery stores, and that's when Merna breaks into her routine. Most often with the company of Joe, much to his horror. Just close your eyes and picture an 86-year-old stripper with her stockings rolled down around her ankles, a pronounced limp, from her hip replacement surgery, a pair of cataract surgery sunglasses, blue hair tint, and a toothless pucker that reminds you of someone trying to suck a tennis ball through a garden hose.

One time while they were at a Price Chopper, Joe was in an isle at the far end of the store, on comes the song Tie a Yellow Ribbon. He rushed through the isles in a full gallop, he turned the comer to the produce section, just in time to see the finale, as Merna casts off her depends right into the romaine lettuce section, Needless to say, when it was all over, the only crowd around them were the store manager and police. Everyone else was either hurrying their kids away or moving toward the exit door.

Well there's a multitude of stories about Merna's stripping escapades, one outdoing the other, but few compare to the time Merna wound up in an elevator full of Orthodox Jews with their Zorro hats and curls, long beards and all that. The doors sprang open just as Merna was lassoing one of the senior members with her 44D brazier. What a sight!

Now, Hilda, Joe's wife, refuses to go anywhere alone With Merna. The main reason is Hilda's hook. You see, Hilda was maimed in a fanning accident as a young girl in Austria. Seems her hand got caught in a mule's bridle while her father was castrating it. The mule broke free and dragged poor Hilda for miles through the hillside till it tore her hand off. Doctors were rare in their town in Austria where Hilda grew up. So, after her father stitched up the stump, the town blacksmith fashioned a hook made of an old horseshoe. Well, Hilda the Hook, as she's known about town, grew up on the farm, doing chores that would have made her quite hardy, but inheriting mostly her father's genes, adding some unique characteristics to her, she stands about 6'2" and weighs in about 230 pounds. She has a somewhat craggy complexion, due to a severe case of chicken pox as a child. Sometime in her 40's, she incurred some sort of hormonal imbalance that caused her voice to deepen and she started sprouting hair under her chin and on her knuckles. Additionally, is a pronounced twitch which causes her to reach to her face as if to scratch. Of course, it's on the hook side, nearly caused her an eye injury several times, to the point now, where on eye is always looking downward. One can only imagine what would happen if Hilda was left to help Merna put her clothes back on in a hurry, most likely in a public place. By the time it was over, someone would need stitches.

Joe, himself, was not particularly attractive, but then what did you expect? He's about 5'3", 190 pounds. Usually dressed in a t-shirt and tuxedo pants, you know, with the satin stripe down the leg. Joe found a box full of tuxedo pants one time during clean-up week (Joe's vacation time) and hasn't had the need to buy pants since.

Joe works at the slaughter house. His job is to stand over the cattle as they come through a stall and smash them over the head with a sledge hammer. On an average shift, Joe usually knocks off about 80 head of cattle or about 10 per hour. Anyone who knows Joe well is certainly aware of his carefree approach to life. I would think his job could be some sort of stress relieving therapy. Joe's the first to admit when he has had a particularly difficult night at home, the next day he's swinging the hammer quite aggressively.

Painting Life with Words of Encouragement

Two weeks ago, Joe and Hilda decided to have a quiet weekend together, including a nice dinner, followed by a live WWF wrestling match at the arena. Well, Joe and Hilda don't get out much, and watching them dine is quite a spectacle to say the least.

Hilda ordered spaghetti, because at home, she discovered it was quite easy to spin on her hook and then suck the spaghetti off the end. Problem is, she's not at home and this antic draws some attention. Then of course there's her twitch, which sends whatever is on the hook in several directions and quite often. Then there was her attire, a brand new, crisp t-shirt, complete with the folds from the bag, bright red and emblazoned across the front "FORTY-FORT MEAT PACKJNG AND PROCESSING." Yep, you guessed it, one of Joe's anniversary presents to Hilda. Coupled with a pair of green spandex at calf length, allowing the hair on her legs just enough exposure to be viewed and a pair of flip flops to show off her size 12 feet, complete with lipstick red nail polish on her hairy toes. She decided at the last minute to wear her long-haired wig, but it needed some refreshing. So, she tossed it in the washer with a load of towels. Between the washing, drying and tangling with the towels, it came out looking like a spider wearing dreadlocks. Going into any greater detail about Hilda's fashion sense would be pointless, I'm sure you could just imagine her make-up, one side applied with her hand and the other with a hook. Try to picture an amorous stare, madame.

Joe's in his usual tuxedo pants Joe and Hilda are fashioning matching shirts. You know, so everyone would understand they were together. They looked like the main act from the wrestling ring. Anyway, Joe's eating pork chops and corn on the cob. His teeth are spaced just right to accumulate as much food as he swallows. On the way out, he sucked enough food through his teeth to have a mouthful by the time they made the door.

Now, they were off to the wrestling match. But first stop is the hotel. You see, the deal is if you stay at this hotel (and I'm not mentioning any names), they have a shuttle straight to the arena and back. Well, they pull into the valet parking area and the first thing the attendant says is, "Deliveries in the rear." And for good reason, Joe's car is in the shop, so the company loaned him a 12' stake body that they use in the cleanup area of the slaughter house.

Need more detail?

Okay then, there is a few years' worth of residue permanently affixed to the truck bed. Some fresher than others, but basically a combination of manure and entrails. Now you get the idea? Maybe not. It's been in the 80's all week. Enough?

So, Joe explains to the attendant, as he hands him the keys, that he and his wife are guests of the hotel, they are in a bit of a hurry and would he get their luggage under the tarp in back.

As the valet moved to get in, Hilda extended her hook to help him up, he was a bit shorter than Joe. She scared the daylights out of him, guess he wasn't expecting it. Hilda laughed so hard, her false teeth flew out and bounced off the dashboard and landed on the valet's lap. The bellhop moved to uncover the luggage just as Joe neared the rear of the truck.

Joe yells, "Not that tarp, the other tarp!" Too late.

The bellhop is now about 20 yards away when he let out a scream. You see, one tarp was covering the luggage, but the other was covering all that Joe shoveled to the corner of the truck bed, tails, hooves, various other body parts, and a pig's head right on top, just starring at him.

Eventually, the commotion settled, and the truck was parked far from anyone else's vehicle.

Hilda and Joe proceeded to check in. The hotel clerk was looking down at his register when Hilda and Joe stepped up. What a start they gave the clerk. The first thing that caught the clerk's attention was an awful smell, a combination of women's cheap perfume, old spice and manure. "What in the name of... Excuse me, ma'am, may I help you?"

"Vee' d like a vroom for da evening please."

"Yes, of course, single or double?

Hilda replies, "Dis is my husband, Joe, and I'm not single, but tanks for askin'."

"Huh? Yes ma'am, would this be for one night or more?" asks the clerk.

"Yon rught please," replies Hilda.

The clerk asks, "Your credit card, ma'am?"

"Of course, it's mine, whose else vood it be?" exclaimed Hilda.

The clerk retorts, "No, you misunderstand, I was asking for your credit card."

"Joseph, give da man your credit card," Hilda instructs Joe.

"Here ya go, buddy."

After Hilda and Joe check in, the bellhop brings their luggage.

They catch the shuttle to the arena, saw the wrestling matches and head back to the hotel. Joe and Hilda blended well with the crowd. Hell, they would have blended wi1h the wrestlers, for that matter.

Back at the hotel parking garage, there seems quite a unique dilemma has arisen. Hotel personnel had to call an animal control officer, the police and a pest control expert. The valet parked the truck nearest the exit. Between the fact the sun was able to shine on it, every cat and dog passing the exit ramp caught a good whiff of the vehicle. The attendant left the windows open, and every imaginable scavenger in the area came in search of the prize. By the time the vehicle was rid of the varmints and chased throughout the parking garage, the interior was trashed.

Apparently, one of the hotel guests entered the parking garage in time to witness several dogs and cats in a feeding frenzy as they uncovered a plastic bag filled with various cattle body parts. One of the most memorable scenes, as related by an elderly couple, was that of 3 dogs in a tug of war with a cow's udder and a dog which appeared to have a tail at both ends. He was carrying one in his mouth, while another dog fought with him the second dog mistook the first dogs' own tail for the one they were fighting over. By the time it was all over, there was animal debris scattered over half the parking deck. There were at least half a dozen individuals running around with nets and snares. Some with dogs still chewing on their prize.

Needless to say, the hotel management had never been trained to deal with the likes of this situation. The kicker was Joe coming to the front desk after having consumed more than enough beer at the wrestling match, attempting to complain about what had been done to his truck's interior, explaining its peculiar cargo.

Well, the combination of Joe's natural lisp and alcohol induced slur, made him virtually incompetent to speak. Now you add to that, Hilda, in the same drunken condition and an Austrian accent and well, what we have here, as the line in the movie, Cool Hand Luke, "Is a failure to communicate."

There was one sentence the hotel manager did understand, it was when Joe and Hilda said they would have to stay another night while they made arrangements to have friends or relatives come to get them, maybe with another truck and tow them back to Forty Fort with a chain. Now, totally flabbergasted and anxious at the thoughts entering his head, the hotel manager snapped, "Oh, no! Uh, that will not be necessary, we will have the vehicle towed and repaired at our expense and we will see to it that you get a ride home."

"In a limousine?" asked Joe.

"In a lim...yes, of course, you'll leave tonight." the manager nervously answered.

Within the hour, Joe and Hilda were checked out. The truck was on a wrecker, and a limo was waiting for its 'special riders'.

This episode ends with not much fanfare. Unless you consider the *grand* exit down the ramp from the parking garage, wrecker with lights flashing, towing a red slop splattered, seat-eaten, stake bodied truck, stray dogs chasing close behind, followed by a ·white stretch limo, Joe waving out the window in a drunken stupor, Hilda waving her hook out the other, and, the hotel staff standing in relieved amazement, as they watched them ride off into the moonlit sky, back to Forty Fort, Pennsylvania.

Till next time, see yaw. De End

Painting Life with Words of Encouragement

Hilda

Joe

Tony Amico

Alone

I have heard it said homes have personalities. I assume most people who say this do not think of this personality in any way other than a figurative sense. But what of the literal personality living, perhaps not occupying a structure, in a spiritual way?

I was in the attic one day in winter, rummaging through some clothes. The air was cold. I was wearing a sweater, but still I was hurrying due to the chill. Suddenly, my back felt warm as if someone had leaned against me from behind, wrapping their arms around my shoulders to comfort me. I was not comforted. No, I was frightened. As I turned, I could feel their breath upon me and a faint smell of perfume. I spun around and saw nothing. I was fully aware that I was not alone.

Now there was a different kind of chill running down my spine. The hair on my back felt like it was standing tall. I tried to mask my fear with anger as I queried aloud, "Who are you?" There was an almost inaudible shuffle to my left. As I turned to face it, the clothing hanging in storage moved, as if someone had just passed through. That was more than I needed to see at that point. I moved quickly to the stairs and down to the door, leading back to the living area. As I closed the door behind me, there was a brief resistance as though someone had passed by me while I completed closing the door. I knew someone was there. I could sense it. And whoever it was, did not want to be alone. By this time, I was wide-eyed but curious. Of one thing I am certain, at this point, femininity resided in this space.

The encounters continued. Sporadically at first, then more often and regular, daringly sensual. The physical contact was increasing in frequency and intensity in a flirtatious and provocative manner.

After she slipped into the living area of the house, I never encountered her in the attic again. It was as if she was afraid to be locked away. Instead, she chose to live with me. There were moments of unusual ability other than her presence, of course. I mean nothing ever flew through the air, no sounds or visual images at least up until this point in the relationship. She never left with me. Once I left the property, she stayed in waiting perpetually nurturing the relationship she initiated. There was an instant when she followed me into the yard, as I sat at the table to read the paper. I remember she was standing behind me, at first, as if she was reading the paper with me. As I scanned the print, I could feel the touch of her hands on my shoulder. When I turned to the obituary page, she abruptly slid her hands off me, like she was disturbed and moved away to somewhere in the yard. I sat there searching for a time, and then moved toward the gate to the house. I closed the gate to the yard behind me and re-entered the house.

That afternoon, I laid down for a nap. I slept maybe an hour and a half. I dreamt of woman named, Sylvia. A loving but promiscuous woman who had an intense love affair with a man, who one day died in his sleep, leaving her alone and heartbroken, and wanting a continuance or a closure to their relationship. The last thing I remembered before awakening was the lost and lonely look on her face as she watched her lover being taken away. As I rose to my feet, it was late afternoon, almost dusk. I peered out the window into the back yard. For a very brief instant, I saw a glimpse of her starring back in the window. She was frightened. I hurried outside, threw open the gate, and felt her rush to me in a panicked embrace. The reality of the moment caused me to lose my balance for an instant and take a step backward. She grasped my arms and held me stead, and then I felt her brush past me toward the door to the house. I followed and as I opened the door, she rushed in before me, pushing me aside.

The doors and gates were somehow her only barrier within this world. As in life, we have no control of the chapters as they open and close. These moments were defined by which door or gate was opened for her to pass through, or closed before her, preventing her journey. This was my only control over her. It was up to me to decide where she would be and for how long.

Was the dream some sort of communication? Telepathy from the other side of life? Somehow, it was soothing to me. Part clarification, part curiosity. Eventually, I would soon discover the link to the answers of many questions surrounding... Sylvia.

Slowly, I stepped inside the house realizing what had transpired. The weirdness of it all. The fear that should have engulfed me. And somehow the curiosity overwhelmed all. I would never have predicted, nor would I be prepared for, what this was leading to.

At first, I began asking questions. I questioned the neighbors about the former owners of the house, checked Courthouse records, friends of the neighbors, and relatives, some of whom moved away years ago. In assembling the bits and pieces, it turns out the original owner of the home I purchased, was indeed a woman named Sylvia. She had a long and intense love affair with a married man. The man built her this house and put it in her name. Something about his wife being unwilling to divorce him or he not wanting to end the marriage for financial reasons. Who knows, it was so long ago. The area, now a small town, was then a series of farms and rural communities. The land where the house is built was acquired through a sub-division of one of these farms, as the area began to change around the turn of the century. The sad twist in Sylvia's life was that shortly after completion of the home, and after a wonderful afternoon together, it was here that her paramour took his final nap from which he never awakened! It is assumed that her relationship with the man was her everything. Her reason for living and her every joy. Afterward, she was never the same. So, where was all this going? Let us not forget this is a ghost we are speaking of. And what kind of purpose does the relationship that is developing serve? Never did I have time to even think it through, at this stage of the game.

There was an encounter or a development at every turn, and all were most significant. I was standing in front of a mirror the first time I really laid eyes on Sylvia. She came from behind me, wrapped her arms around my waist and kissed my neck. I was startled and yet so pleased. Her hair was pulled back and toward the top, as in days of old, circa 1890's. Her dress was pleated and ruffled at the neck. And her face, smooth as silk, a medium complexion with a small beauty mark or mole, if you please, just to the side of her lips. She smiled broadly at me in the mirror. The smell of Lilac perfume filled the air. I turned to face her, and she disappeared. I could still feel her and felt her embrace now around my neck. I could smell her and feel her breath, as would be in life.

She was unseen except when I turned toward the mirror. Only through the eyes of the mirror could she be seen. My distraction in trying to view her in the mirror seemed to confuse or disturb her. It seemed as if only I could see her this way. But to her whether mirror or not, we were seen the same.

She spoke not a word during this encounter. I was both speechless and powerless within her embrace. I pulled back and just as I began to mouth a word of question, she walked into the mirror and vanished into the reflected room. I touched the glass as if I could follow and was now very aware of my existence and inability to join her. A few days passed, I did not see Sylvia or experience any signs that she was here. I began walking around the house holding a hand mirror. If someone ever saw me, they would think I had lost my mind.

A week, then two weeks, nothing… I tried to convince myself I was no longer looking for her, that she had gone on to somewhere else. I couldn't help but question, *Where was she? Why had she appeared in the first place? What had I hoped for? Was this a relationship? Was I really losing my mind? Did I imagine this?*

One day after many weeks, I was sitting on the edge of the bed thinking, remembering and talking aloud how I came to be in this house. A few years prior, after taking my retirement from a twenty-five-year Marine Corp career, I had settled in Norfolk, Virginia, with a woman I had dated in the last years of my military life. Her name was, June. We were just right for each other. Both of us athletic, we enjoyed the theater, art exhibits, went to church on Sundays, fished on Sunday afternoons, sometimes into the evening. We dined out, drank fine wine, and even enjoyed being apart for short afternoons. We always met up later and rarely fell asleep other than in each other's arms.

Most of my friendships were military buddies. Our get togethers after retirement were always planned, due to distance. So, June and I became both lovers and friends. She had little family and no real ties to her hometown of Fairfax. I asked June to marry me on Christmas Eve, 2001. I bought her a nice ring. We began making plans for a Spring wedding. We booked a fancy hotel ballroom, hired a great caterer, and a top-notch band, everything and anything that would add to a fairytale wedding.

The weeks and months leading to our wedding day flew by. Two days before the wedding, I was cooking a meal for the two of us (one of my past times), set the table with candlelight, chilled the wine, and couldn't wait for her to come in and say that familiar, "Hey baby, like wow!"

I remember laughing as I opened the door to receive her, but my laughter cracked to a smile, followed by a poker straight face, matching my expression was the police officer standing at my door holding June's ID card, listing me as the person to notify in the event of an emergency. "Dear God, please don't tell me…"

Never finishing the sentence, the officer interrupted, "Are you Colonel Pierce?"

"Yes, I am Dave Pierce, what's happened?" I asked as I grasped both of his arms as if to shake the information from him.

"There's been an accident, a terrible accident. Could I step inside?"

"Yeah, please, come in. What happened?"

"The woman, June—"

"My fiancé," I interrupted.

"She hit a deer about a mile and half from here, I guess she got out of the car to see if there was anything she could do to help the animal. It's raining and there's a heavy fog. The oncoming traffic was unable to avoid her in time, she was struck by two cars, one driving her into the path of another. She was killed instantly."

I grew numb, unable to respond. I just shook my head, stepped backwards to a chair, and sat crying out the word "No!"

All I had looked forward to had ended in an instant of compassion. It was like her to put anything or anyone before herself or her own safety. But so hard to accept or internalize.

When I went to make the positive identification, there was little resemblance to the woman I held in my arms just the night before. I held the hand that I placed the engagement ring on. She was cold, so cold. God how I wished I could turn back the clock. I felt as if I were wandering in a foreign place, surrounded by misery.

I raised my head from my hands, realizing I was speaking aloud, as if relating the story to someone. I was face to face with the mirror. Sylvia was there looking in my eyes. She was crying.

She reached out to comfort me but I touched only glass this time, as if she had imprisoned herself. She remained in the reflected room. I was again, alone.

Gently, she reached out to me, as I took her hand, she entered the room, disappearing as she exited the mirror, though present to my touch and senses. She walked behind me as in the past encounters and looked compassionately into the mirror, and my eyes, as we locked on each other's gaze. "You heard everything?"

She nodded affirmatively.

"We share a common loss."

Tears streamed down her face, and she nodded once more.

"Speak to me, why can't I hear the sound of your voice? Please, speak to me!"

She drew close to my ear. I could feel her breath upon me, the scent of lilacs filling the room. Then she whispered, "Eternity awaits me. Our time is fleeting, and the end draws near. Each moment is but a gift of stolen time. Forgive me."

"Forgive what, Sylvia?" I asked.

She was gone.

When I left Virginia, it was a necessary move. I had to leave behind the dreams that turned to nightmares. The future, which turned to a depressing present. So, I moved north to Pennsylvania, in search of a new start at this state of mid-life. Who would have dreamed I could have stepped into this twisted torment with someone I dare not speak about to anyone? Her imprisonment is now shared with me in such a cruel manner.

Over the next few weeks and months, I accepted our situation. Though the underlying element was ever increasing. It was the element of passion. For some reason, there was always a cutoff point with her. We had numerous physical encounters. Being a man in this weird relationship, increased my frustration as well as my curiosity, and finally my lust for what should not be.

Something in Sylvia's response to me was forewarning.

By now, the shock of seeing her ghostly presence had become normalcy. I was a lonely man and she was a tormented soul. Each of us in need of something only the other could provide. Both of us wanting more of each other. Fully aware of the obvious, but there were far more serious questions to be answered. I lacked the capability to resolve them without her verbal input. The lack of conversation was indeed perplexing at the least. We looked at each other longingly now. A wanting lust that only consummation could satisfy. And yet, each time it seemed as though it would progress to that moment, she would avoid me by exiting in her ghostly style. Always. As if she feared the result of such a cross between our two worlds. It would be an understatement to say what we had was unique. The positive elements of this macabre relationship were precious.

At my lowest moments, she was there to comfort me as only she could do. She was pleasing to my eyes. Especially when she was disrobed from her Victorian era attire. I would amuse her with my mannerisms and sometimes quirky responses. I was, in fact, fulfilling an element of a relationship she longed for with an unmarried man. Someone who did not have to go home to his wife. I ignored what we could not share, a walk together in a park or on a city street, friendships with others, dining together. It's humorously painful.

The relationship reached a point where most would have, in a shorter period of time, except for a wonderful aspect, we grew to know each other long before we desired each other. There was a look conveyed between us that only the intensely in love possess. No matter who was the pursuer, either of us was a willing prey. But we were damned by the bounds of life. That is a reality no one could be prepared for. To compound matters, was the lack of dialog between us. There were limitations to her abilities to perform among the living, no matter how real it all seemed.

Whenever the intensity escalated, there was a period of absence. I do not know if she was responsible for this or if there is a controlling force preventing our interaction beyond a certain point. Whatever the case, each and every time we were drawn to the point of consummation, she would fearfully pull away and be gone for an extended period of time. Such is the case now, as I'm conveying this in writing. It has been weeks since I have had any contact. I am becoming reclusive and resistant to anyone and everyone close to me. All this time, everyone is in the dark with regard to Sylvia. Whom would I talk to that would not think I had gone crazy? What an existence.

So, I end another day in this my chosen--perhaps not--imprisonment. Retiring to my bed at 12:30 am, it is a Thursday.

Sometime around 3:30 am, I am awakened by movement in my bed. You would think I would be used to this sort of thing by now. I sprang to me feet, turned on the light and there before me was Sylvia's form framed by the covers. Pulling the covers back, the scent of lilacs was everywhere. I rushed to grab the hand mirror and view her in all her naked splendor. She smiled and reached for me to join her. Off went the light and into her waiting embrace. In the darkness, you see with your senses. I was on fire in every way. Grasping her arms nearest her shoulders, I spun her over on top of me. I delighted in feeling her long hair cascade onto my face. Her warm body pressed to mine. Her breath panting softly in my ear. We rolled once more. I lay with my elbows supporting me as I drew deeply inhaling her scent. She sighed and whispered to me, "Please."

We kissed as if never a kiss could be filled with such passion. Thrashing and pawing, I felt her teeth graze my neck at the base of my shoulder. I moved to complete the consummation. It was amazing, to say the least. As if she controlled my stamina. I thought we could go on endlessly. I remember thinking that if this was the last time we made love, I would live with the memory of a lifetime. She pulled to my ear and exhaustingly said to me, "I'm so sorry David, the end has come. One day, we will meet again on the other side of life."

Her voice weakened and faded as we reached the pinnacle of ecstasy. And suddenly she was gone beneath me, vanishing, leaving only her aroma. I searched with my hands in every direction of the bed. I reached for the light switch, she was gone. There I stood, bewildered and cheated of those last moments that would have meant so much to me.

It was winter now, as cold and brutal as it could be. One evening her voice filled the rooms of my tiny house, but in a whisper, as on that last encounter, she called my name. This time, it seemed to beckon me towards the door and outside. I grabbed my coat and hat and walked out into the night air. It was a moonlit sky. The air was still and crisp. Though it was cold, it was pleasant. I walked for miles toward her beckoning and entered the grounds of a cemetery. Past rows of tombstones and monuments, I approached an area that would be overgrown in summer, an abandoned spot of ground with stones worn with age. Most of the tombstones were illegible or broken. Some were toppled, others half buried. Sylvia's voice had stopped calling me. I stood in complete silence, albeit a passing breeze. As I took a half turn, I spotted a heart-shaped stone carved of pink granite. I approached slowly and knelt to read its inscription:

"*I was like the Lilac in spring, brief.*"

Beneath the phrase was the surname, Valentine, Sylvia, Died January 5, 1893, Age 29 years.

"That's it?" I yelled aloud, " Is this all there is?"

"I'm here on the other side now."

I walked in circles, paced so many feet away and then back to the grave. Staring blankly at the stone, skyward to God, pleading for something that was so wrong and yet so much what I needed. Finally, I walked away and back home.

As I entered the front door, I was immediately confronted by her absence. I knew she was gone and would never return to this life. Sylvia was at rest now. Her restless soul was now at peace. It was I who was left in a tormented despair. I was left wandering the rooms of the prison created by her lack of existence. I began walking to the gravesite every day, sometimes twice a day. Mainly in the late evening with no regard to the weather conditions. Rain, snow, cold, into the dead of winter.

I am a recluse now. Unshaven, unkempt and alone. Alone with my thoughts, alone with my agony. She completed me even with all that was missing. When I gaze into the mirror now, all around me is as empty as the look in my eyes. "Where are you? Why can't you...please, please..."

This was David's last entry. It was a cold morning in February. February 14th, 2007, he was found face down at Sylvia's grave. The journal held tightly to his chest. A hand mirror lay next to him, apparently smashed by his battered fist. His fingernails torn and scrapped to the tips of his fingers as he obviously scratched at the frozen ground. An empty bottle of cognac lay next to him. As he was turned over, one could not help but notice the peaceful smile frozen on his face, as if he finely reached his objective.

To those who may wonder who completed David's journal, it is a question best left unanswered. But the entries as penned by David's hand are intact and descriptive. Their accuracy may only be verified by the two principals involved. They are the two most affected by this outcome.

Painting Life with Words of Encouragement

VALENTINE SYLVIA
DIED JAN 5, 1893
AGED 29 YRS.

Her Companion: Colonel David Pearce
Died – February 14th, 2007
Age 52 years

About the Author

Anthony "Tony" Amico was born in 1957 to first generation Italian American parents, Anthony and Angela Delfino-Amico. His two siblings, sister, Joann and brother, Sam, have seven years between them. In his words, "My parents apparently believed in spacing us out. It was as if we all were an only child."

Tony was raised in a predominately Italian-American neighborhood on a dead-end street. The street was his playground. Anyone driving in from outside the neighborhood, were immediately identified as a stranger.

Many of the grandparents lived in the same household, in those days.

The same aroma in various varieties emanated from our kitchens. Especially, on Sunday mornings before church. Fried meatballs, red sauce and the unmistakable and intoxicating smell of garlic. Everyone's home had its own influences. Whether to emulate or perhaps to resist, but all were learning experiences, to say the least.

Where most kids had chores to do to earn their allowance, Tony's parents weren't so regimented with their children. He earned his tips from running bets for his father to the various neighborhood bookies. They had 'off track betting' long before it was legal. Horse race bets, card games, dice, and numbers racket were commonplace.

Tony remembers standing behind his dad in a smoke-filled room of poker or pinochle players, waiting for a few winning hands from him or his friends to slide him a quarter or 50 cents. It was a cash cow for 7 or 8-year-old. It would never happen today!

He was always artistic. Tony could draw, sculpt and paint as far back as he could remember. Writing would come later in life. His childhood memories colored his thoughts as they still do.

He often referred to growing up in an *enchanted* neighborhood. Houses close together, all the parents watching out for all the kids. Most moms were stay at home. Deliverymen were hucksters, the milkman and peddlers, the ragman, often referred to as the sheeney.

Tony grew up fast. His mom was ever nurturing, his dad the disciplinarian. Tony's sister and brother were like his second parents. He was always aware of outside influences and experiences. Although, there were some shortcomings, there were opportunities many of his friends didn't have. He's sure the same was true to them of him. From the time he was 11 until around 16, he spent a great deal of his summer vacations in New Jersey riding horses on his cousin's ranch. No one from his neighborhood rode horses. He felt very special and has a heartfelt appreciation for horses, to this day. Tony started working at age 15, during the Wilkes Barre, Pennsylvania Flood of 1972, his dad was his foreman. Tony felt his father to be a good boss. Looking back now, it may have been their closest time other than when adversity entered.

High school wasn't fun for Tony. It was something he couldn't wait for to end. He felt he wasn't college minded and regrets never having enlisted with the Marines. Tony knows he would have made a good soldier. By the time he was 20, he was a married, with one child of his own, Michelangelo. Yes, he was named after the artist. Tony wasn't prepared for the responsibility and the marriage failed within five years. Tony gained custody and took responsibility for raising their son. Michel's mom, Nancy and Tony were in agreement that being with Tony would be best. He did what may have been, to the best of his ability, but Tony feels he surely fell short in many regards as a parent. You don't get a second chance.

Tony remarried a few years later trying to bring some normalcy back into their lives. All was not as it seemed. His marriage was better for Tony than for Michel. The turmoil of life took a tragic turn on Wednesday, August 25th around 5pm when Michel used Tony's pistol to take his own life, at the age of 14. Tony's life would be forever changed. It took a long time to continue, unsaddled with this incredible experience.

The vision of Tony's last time with his son, just hours before, and ending with finding Michel this way, haunted him for months afterward. It was during a heart to heart with God that this vision was eased. And it became a road to witness to others of God's communication with Tony.

Tony began to write more as a form of self-therapy. As if writing to himself, the writer was and is often his alter ego. It's the honesty Tony feels he, himself, needs to hear. As if it were two people. One - the person who is writing. The other - the one who needs to hear the message. Perhaps as reflection, justification or confirmation of the reaction to life's ever-changing directions and experiences.

In time, others began to notice and referred to his ability as a fit. He states, "We all have gifts. And we should not only be grateful, but we are meant to share them. After the events of the 1990's, my writing increased to a point where I had to stop whatever I was doing, to record a thought that I would follow up on later."

By the time Tony met his wife, Valerie, there was obviously a body of work. After her introducing him to social media, he began to attract a following.

Eventually, at the encouragement of others, most significantly Valerie and a dear friend, Laura Summa, Tony began what is contained within the pages of this book. And hopefully others to follow.

Tony hopes to use this book as a vehicle to personally reach out to others. Focusing primarily on those who have contemplated suicide, and those who have been affected by a tragic death of a loved one.

Tony knows he is not a therapist and has nothing but this gift, instinct and experience to use to a positive end. And so, if in some way large or small, something he has written helps you feel better, amuses you, or just causes you to look at life from a positive perspective, then Tony feels he has hopefully fulfilled a purpose and prays that God will use him in His own way to that end.

Tony supposes why someone writes is not any easier to explain than why someone draws, paints or sculpts. Although artistic ability and expression are gifts, and gifts are meant to be enjoyed, cared for and especially shared, Tony knows he has been blessed artistically speaking, and has delved into many mediums of creativity. But writing is by far, the most therapeutic, ever-evolving, revealing reflection of himself.

Tony will be eternally grateful for the ability to express, and the gift of coloring other's lives in any way God wants him to.

Life can't be explained. It is perfection and imperfection as though one in the same. And he writes as though he is exploring every facet. It soothes his soul and purges his thoughts, as if being released from a faucet. When he writes it's as if the thoughts need to be freed immediately, and when the thought is completed, the spigot is closed. For now.

Above all, Tony hopes you enjoy!

More from Foundations

Seasons and Sentiments *Maron Craig Bielovitz*
Embracing a broad range of subjects, styles and moods, this book of contemporary poetry represents nearly a lifetime of the poetry composed by Maron Craig Bielovitz. Always in tune with nature and the seasons around her, Maron has brought those impressions to life here while also sharing some of her personal photographs taken along the way. Rhyming, free verse, somber, sentimental, alliterative and just plain fun verses are here for readers of all ages.

Shattered Living *Justice K. Chambers*
Justice K. Chambers' debut work, Shattered Living, touches on the fragility and darkness of the human state when suffering with mental illness. In this collection of fifty-two poems, she takes the reader on an eye-opening journey of inner turmoil and loss of self, then brings them to a place of acceptance, where they can learn to cope and find their light in the shadows again. May not be suitable for YA.

Accept the Broken Heart *Robin Leigh Anderson*
 What can be said of Hell, when at its most quiet, I was most terrified? The explosions had rocked every fiber of my being and made my bones feel like they could simply shatter like tempered glass still resonated.
 I looked over at the wounded, wondering if I had the same haunted look in my eyes, and thought I probably did. In this war, no one leaves. No one goes home...and everyone is a casualty of war.

Made in the USA
Columbia, SC
01 September 2018